To Mason —
I'm always thinkin
you up — I hope you
book. You are m
and that's in the bible.
Start with reading chapt. 1 page 1 — Self-esteem.

THINK HAPPY THOUGHTS AFFIRMATIONS AND MEDITATION FOR POSITIVE THINKING, LEARNED OPTIMISM AND A HAPPY BRAIN

Love
mom
5/13/20

Unlock the Advantage of the Happiness Habit
and Project the Power of Positive Energy

Congrats on the Honor Roll
& IF you Believe it — You can Achieve it!

DREW MCARTHUR *— Jesse Jackson*

All by Drew McArthur on
Amazon & Audible

Affirmations, Meditation, & Hypnosis For Positivity & A Success Mindset:

Power Of Thought To Create A Millionaire Mind, Manifest Wealth, Abundance, Better Relationships, & Form Positive Habits Now

Rewire Your Brain Affirmations, Meditation, & Hypnosis For Confidence, Motivation, & Discipline:

Increase Focus, Productivity, Willpower, Self Esteem, & Eliminate Distraction & Procrastination Habits

Step-By-Step Motivational Goal Setting Course For Life Mastery:

How To Change Your Brain, Set Your Vision, And Get Everything You Want To Have Your Best Year Ever

Monkey Mind Cure Affirmations, Meditation & Hypnosis:

How to Stop Worrying, Kill Fear, Rewire Your Brain, and Change Your Anxious Thoughts to Start Living a Stress and Anxiety-Free Life

Think Happy Thoughts: Affirmations and Meditation for Positive Thinking, Learned Optimism and a Happy Brain

Unlock the Advantage of the Happiness Habit and Project the Power of Positive Energy

Millionaire Money Mindset: Affirmations, Meditation, & Hypnosis

Using Positive Thinking Psychology to Train Your Mind to Grow Wealth, Think like the New Rich and Take the Secret Fastlane to Success

Contents

Introduction

Have you ever been around people who enter a room and just light it up with their energy, and people gravitate towards them and just love having them around for reasons they can't quite put their finger on? Ever been in a room where someone walks in, and immediately the mood drops and changes in a way that's palpable, yet hard to explain? Have you noticed how some people just seem to be happy all the time no matter what is thrown at them? Do you know someone who always has some sort of crisis and there is always something going wrong or falling apart in their life and everyone and everything is just always against them?

If you have had the privilege to travel the world, you know first-hand that some of the most impoverished people, living in the most dire of circumstances are blissfully happy. Yet, close to home, you see rich people who seem to have it all, and are hopelessly miserable. Happiness is not about what happens outside of you. It is about what is happening *inside* of you.

Your mindset makes all the difference. Disempowering thoughts can make you feel helpless, and hopeless. And these negative thoughts are often rooted in our subconscious, so we don't even realize the psychological damage we're doing to ourselves. But training your brain to be positive, optimistic, and expect good things to happen to you and for you, can be the difference between seeing success, and not seeing success.

A successful life is a happy life. And a happy life is a successful life—however you choose to define success. But it all begins (and ends) in the mind—shaping and training it to think how you want it to think.

One very effective way to do this is by using affirmations. Affirmations can quite literally rewire your mind, by physically affecting the neural pathways in your brain. Affirmations, when spoken coupled with the feeling one would feel if they honestly believed them to be true, can be extremely powerful tools in improving and changing your life.

If you have the habit of happy thoughts and a happy disposition, you will find it easy to be happy no matter your circumstances, and it will be easy for you to bounce back from times of trouble. You'll also find that the happier you get, the more good things will happen to you. And if you do not develop a habit of happiness and optimism, you will find that happiness will always elude you no matter how great your life circumstances may be. And the more negatively you look at the things around you, the worse things will become.

Each day of life is a gift meant to be treasured and enjoyed, yet most people go through life simply waiting for each day to end, as if life itself is a burden. Happiness does not always come naturally to everyone. Happiness is a habit. Happiness is a choice. We cannot always choose what happens, but we can choose our response and we can choose our thoughts around what happens. And optimism and happiness are always a better choice than pessimism and misery.

It's time to reclaim your mental peace, get

back your joy, and attract positive things into your life. It's time to get the rock solid foundation in place to get through life seeing the glass half full.

This audio features affirmations in the following categories in this order.

- Self-esteem
- Success
- Accentuating the Positive
- Relationships & Supporting Others
- Gratitude
- Optimism
- Healthy Happy Habits, Healthy Happy Life

Some sections are a little bit shorter than others. So you can select the chapter of your choice based on what you have time for at that given time. Or you can listen straight through all chapters. Because this is designed for audio and continuous listening, there is no conclusion for this audiobook.

Now, let's see how you can make the most out of this audio…

You can use this audiobook as affirmations, meditation, or hypnosis. If you choose to use it as affirmations, I suggest that you pick a time and a place where you will feel completely confident speaking each affirmation out loud. Maybe for you, that's your bathroom in front of your mirror before bed every night. Maybe it's your living room when the kids are away at soccer practice. Maybe it's your car on your commute on your way to work. No matter where you choose to recite your affirmations, remember that the whole point of this is to ingrain positive, strong thoughts in your head. So, make sure your body language reflects that also. Depending upon where you are, stand up straight, or sit up straight while you speak each statement aloud. Make sure your shoulders are back and your head is up. The confidence in your body needs to be in alignment with the confidence in your words and thoughts in order for this to work. You cannot speak powerful statements and think positive thoughts, while having a slumped, unconfident, disempowered posture in your body.

If you would like to use this as meditation, before you begin, find a quiet place where you will remain undisturbed for the entire length of the audio. Then, remove all distractions. Turn off your phone, eliminate as much noise as possible, close the door to where ever you are, and alert anyone around you not to disturb you for the next two hours. When you're ready to begin, find a comfortable position, either sitting up or laying down, and be sure to remove all physical tension from your body. Choose a position that is comfortable enough for you to allow the muscles of your body to relax, but that will also ensure that you stay awake. Many people like to sit with their legs crossed and their hands resting palm up or down on their knees. Some people prefer to lay down on their backs, with their arms palms up, by their sides. Choose whichever is best for you. Then, once you are settled into position, you can either choose a spot to look at and drop your eyelids and soften your gaze, or you can close your eyes altogether. Then, begin clearing your mind of all past, present, and future thoughts and worries, and deepen your relaxed state by slowing your breathing to long, deep breaths, fully inhaling, then fully exhaling. When you feel you are adequately relaxed, begin the audio. If you like, you can just listen to the audio and let the words seep into your mind and your consciousness, or you can repeat them in your head during the pauses.

Lastly, if you would like to use this as hypnosis, simply start the audio and let it play when you go to bed, allowing the words to embed themselves into your subconscious as you fall asleep.

It doesn't matter how you choose to use this audio, as all of the methods can be effective for you, and make a noticeable difference in your default state of mind and your future success. The ideal scenario may even be to use a combination of all three. That way, you can not only consciously absorb these thoughts, but you can also simultaneously subconsciously absorb them as well. The most important thing is to be consistent. Whatever you do, make sure you do it every day—even multiple times a day if you have time. You can begin your day with affirmations, and end it with meditation and hypnosis. But just keep doing it. Change will not happen overnight. It will take time to reprogram your mind for success, but I assure you, it will be well worth the effort.

Don't worry about looking or sounding weird to other people. Don't worry about what other people may think of you. Whenever you feel strange or uncomfortable about doing this, just remember why you are doing this and think about your goals. If you need help setting goals, I have a program available on Audible that can help you with that task.

I also have several other affirmations audio programs that will help you continue your quest towards habitual positive thinking. So be sure to check out my other titles on Audible and Amazon.

And now, let us begin. Welcome to the next step in becoming a better, happier, more effective version of yourself. Are you ready?

Self-esteem

1. I have the ability to accomplish anything that I set my mind to.
2. I believe that my future is bright and that things will work out for the best for me.
3. I believe in myself and my abilities.
4. I triumph over my mistakes.
5. I learn from each experience to improve myself and do better next time.
6. I radiate positive energy, and my

unwavering enthusiasm helps benefit others.

7. I have an engaging and warm personality that draws people to want to be around me.

8. I have the conviction to follow through on my beliefs.

9. I celebrate my uniqueness and individuality instead of comparing myself to others.

10. I am confident and secure in myself no matter what others think.

11. I possess the confidence to take charge of my own life.

12. I am generous and giving, and take other people's best interest into consideration.

13. I prioritize my long term happiness over instant gratification.

14. I have full faith and trust in myself to make the right decisions.

15. I am at my best when I think happy thoughts and push negative emotions to the side.

16. I am at my best when I believe in myself.

17. I am at my best when I persevere to finish the task before me.

18. I motivate and encourage others to believe in themselves.

19. Whenever I see someone who has achieved something that I want, I see it as inspiration and evidence that I can achieve the same.

20. I conquer my fears and turn them into strengths.

21. I deserve happiness and success because I am a good person.

22. Regardless of my ambitions, I pursue my goals with morality and ethics.

23. I value myself as a person because I have strong character traits of honesty and integrity.

24. I participate in activities that I enjoy to bring happiness into my life.
25. I gladly take on challenges to further increase my self-confidence and boost my self-esteem.
26. I confront my personal demons and turn them around with self-awareness and positive action.
27. I love doing kind things for others because it makes us both happier.
28. I treat myself kindly because I know I am worthy of respect.
29. I love and appreciate what my body does for me, so I pay attention to what I feed it.
30. I possess skills and talents that other people could benefit from.
31. I possess the will and the resourcefulness to change things in my life for the better.
32. I am an authentic and genuine

person, capable of speaking my
mind fearlessly.

33. I treat others with respect and
surround myself with people who
treat me with respect.

34. I am a beautiful person, and I
respect myself by taking care of
my body and my mind.

35. I possess the stamina and
endurance to persevere in my
pursuits.

36. I am confident and assertive at all
times regardless of what other
people may think.

37. I am constantly getting to know
myself better and improve my
areas of weakness.

38. I deserve to feel happy because
I'm worth it and I matter.

39. Before I can love others, I must
first learn to truly and fully love
and appreciate myself.

40. It is easy for me to love others

because I unconditionally love
myself.

41. I make it a priority to be kind to
    myself.
42. I have control over my effort, and
    always put my best foot forward.
43. I take care of my outer appearance
    because the confidence that causes
    makes me feel better on the inside.
44. I have the willpower to take a
    break from outside influences like
    social media if I find myself
    comparison shaming.
45. My opinion matters, even if it is
    unpopular.
46. I have the courage to speak my
    mind on subjects that are
    important to me.
47. The way I see others is a reflection
    of the way I see myself.
48. I am better because of the tight
    knit bonds I have with my friends
    and family.

49. I feel attractive and confident.
50. I walk into every room with a confident posture.
51. I constantly take note of my talents and abilities to remind myself that I am capable of accomplishing anything.
52. I take time to celebrate my achievements and highlight my successes.
53. I am a loyal and genuine person, and anyone would be lucky to have a relationship with me.
54. I have a good sense of humor and the ability to make people smile and laugh.
55. I care for my body with consistent physical exercise because it makes me feel positive about myself.
56. I am a selfless and generous person.
57. I take time to volunteer to help those less fortunate than me.

58. I forgive others because the act of forgiveness is empowering.
59. I possess the potential and the drive to succeed, and I am worthy of success.
60. I am the kind of person who is destined for success and greatness.
61. I speak kind words to myself and remind myself that I can do well and succeed.
62. I evaluate my progress and success based on what *I* am doing, not what other people are doing.
63. I am a patient and empathetic person who other people love to be around.
64. I achieve tiny victories every day that I celebrate and commend myself for.
65. I value myself enough to choose to spend time only with people who love me for who I am.

66. I only have people in my life who appreciate my uniqueness.
67. I accept myself with all my imperfections, and I work to improve myself every day.
68. I channel all negativity and turn it into something positive.
69. I possess the courage to keep trying even if I do not succeed the first time around.
70. I have the self-discipline to deliver on all of my promises.
71. My self-esteem allows me to reflect on my previous triumphs and motivate me towards new accomplishments.
72. I have limitless potential to succeed and become the best version of myself.
73. I always come out a stronger and better person when I face and overcome adversity.
74. I focus on the present and

improving myself for the future, rather than dwelling on the past.

75. I always cultivate feelings of gratitude.
76. I stay mindful of all the happiness I have in my life.
77. I wake up excited every morning, grateful to live another day.
78. I am grateful for the opportunity to become my best self and live my best life.
79. I am always in tune with what my body, mind, and gut are telling me.
80. I set aside personal time to engage in activities I enjoy because it makes me feel happy.
81. My space is an expression of who I am, and it reflects my individuality, and my cheerful mood.
82. I proudly display personal items and awards in my space that

remind me of my accomplishments.

83. I am enthusiastic about life, which fuels my motivation.

84. I am strong in my will, and I am able to overcome any temporary setbacks.

85. I constantly put effort into becoming happy on the inside because I know that turns into success on the outside.

86. I possess strong desire and determination—two key factors in creating success.

87. I confidently and happily invest in myself because I know I have what it takes to succeed.

88. I have a positive and inclusive worldview.

89. I am accepting of all people's differences, choices, and opinions.

90. I am proud of my positive personal attributes.

91. I always keep my past achievements at top of mind to keep myself encouraged.
92. An optimistic attitude is part of my identity.
93. I am brave and determined enough to keep pushing forward, even through difficult times.
94. I am mentally and emotionally strong enough to adapt to change with ease and flexibility.
95. I deserve the opportunity to have a rich, fulfilling life.
96. I have excellent critical thinking and problem solving abilities that serve me well in my life and work.
97. I take control over transforming my life because I believe in myself.
98. My positive thinking contributes to positive growth.
99. I have the dignity and self-confidence to always be true to myself.

100. I am proud of my individual uniqueness, as that is what defines me and makes me special.
101. I have a gift of finding the bright side in every situation.
102. My sunny disposition constantly attracts people who improve the quality of my life.
103. I am constantly making progress in my emotional control, emotional development, and emotional intelligence.
104. I have the conviction that my dreams are worthwhile and should be pursued.
105. I am dedicated enough to put forth maximum effort until I become successful.
106. I have the self-control to reject any unhealthy impulses.
107. I have the maturity to see people and situations purely for what they

are, and not take anything
personally.

108. I am a positive role model for
myself and others.

109. I am optimistic person, with an
optimistic mind, heart, and spirit.

110. I have the willpower to resist
temptations that do not help me in
becoming the best version of
myself.

111. I only compare myself to myself
and not to others.

112. I have the courage to do the right
thing in any situation.

113. I have the power to control my
own level of happiness.

114. I love and accept myself, and it
inspires others around me to do
the same.

115. I remain encouraged and persist
with a positive attitude in the face
of difficulty.

116. I am confident in my ability to find

new ways of doing things if
necessary.

117. I have the courage to take risks
and put myself out there.

118. I have the strength of character to
let small things go and always be
the bigger person.

119. I am the gatekeeper of my own
mind, and I only grant access to
positivity.

120. I have the will to change my
circumstances when things are not
going well.

121. When I want something different,
I have the willpower to do
something different.

122. I deserve to have hopes and
dreams to pursue.

123. I am certain that happiness and
success are in my future.

124. I have the patience required to
make continuous life
improvements.

125. I am a good-natured person, and I do not allow negativity to drag me down.
126. I have the self-compassion to not be overly critical of myself.
127. I am comfortable with giving and receiving compliments and praise.
128. I am secure enough to discuss my viewpoints and experiences with my peers without shame or fear of judgment.
129. I have the individuality to make my own decisions and take responsibility for them.
130. I have valuable opinions to contribute, and I share them with others.
131. I choose to give more attention to my strengths than my weaknesses.
132. My high self-esteem allows me to build strong, long-lasting personal and professional relationships.

133. I am at peace with who I am inside and out.
134. I incorporate physical and mental practices into my daily life that promote positivity and combat negativity.
135. I have the resolve to keep growing and bettering myself every day.
136. I am worthy of being loved by people romantically and platonically.
137. I have the willpower to reshape my thoughts into an optimistic outlook.
138. I proudly and boldly create my own unique identity and don't care what other people think about me.

Success

1. I am constantly working hard and building my skill set to advance my professional success.
2. I do not measure my success by the amount of money I earn, but by my quality of life.
3. I do not measure my success by the amount of money I earn, but the quality of people with which I surround myself.
4. I have a healthy work-life balance that promotes my mental and emotional health.

5. I show initiative and dedication by arriving to work early every day.

6. I always do my best in every situation and motivate others through my dedication to excellence.

7. I possess the resiliency and fortitude to recover from my mistakes and move forward.

8. I enhance my life with hobbies and leisure activities outside of work that make me happy.

9. I have the courage and the capability to conquer all challenges that come my way.

10. I easily remain focused on completing my daily tasks.

11. I always have opportunities to be successful because I do my best.

12. I challenge myself to improve a little each day, which increases my chances of success.

13. I do not allow the fear of failure to stop me from chasing my dreams.
14. I dress for success because presenting a good appearance makes me feel good.
15. I put effort into my appearance so I can always give a good first impression.
16. I practice the skills I want to hone a little each day, so I become more proficient.
17. I cast a wide net and broaden my horizons to explore the various available opportunities.
18. I set realistic and achievable goals for myself that I am accomplishing with ease and happiness.
19. I constantly expand my knowledge by learning more every day through reading and research.
20. I have the willpower and self-control to finish tasks even when they present challenges or stress.

21. I possess the wisdom and the courage to make decisions that will improve my life.
22. I experience more success in my career when I possess a positive attitude.
23. I am consciously creating a happy, well-rounded, and productive life for myself.
24. My physical performance is at a peak when my mental performance is also.
25. I focus on being happy, which is a key factor in achieving success.
26. I do not quantify my success by the material possessions I own, but by the happiness that I feel.
27. I seek out interesting side projects that help keep my mind happy and productive outside of work.
28. I ensure my personal happiness first and foremost, and as a result, personal success easily follows.

29. I possess strong leadership qualities.
30. I have the capacity to make a positive impact in this world.
31. I am always learning, always growing, and always improving in every area of my life.
32. I love what I do for a living and my career makes me genuinely happy.
33. I have the drive to follow through on my ideas and finish what I start.
34. I invest my time and energy into focusing on the steps needed to achieve my goals.
35. I am successful, resourceful, and efficient because I focus on solutions instead of dwelling on problems.
36. I constantly expose myself to new ideas, unique viewpoints, and

different ways of approaching
situations.

37. I am complementary and
supportive of those who I work
with.

38. I choose to focus on solving
problems and finding solutions.

39. I effortlessly feed my body only
with things that make me feel
good, productive, and mentally
alert.

40. Everything I put in my body
makes me feel healthier and
happier in life and work.

41. I have a clear vision and always
maintain sight of my goals.

42. I easily come up with action plans
to accomplish my goals
successfully and effortlessly.

43. Whenever I'm faced with a
problem I cannot yet solve, a
mentor appears to help me
through.

44. I solicit the counsel of experienced people who help guide me on the right path.
45. I take pride in maintaining a professional, put together appearance.
46. I have control over the urge to procrastinate.
47. I effortlessly meet deadlines in a timely manner without stress or anxiety.
48. A significant part of my personal success is giving back to others in a positive, impactful way.
49. I communicate well with the people that I work with.
50. All of my goals are within my reach.
51. I always seek the opportunity to learn and grow more within my field.
52. I am grateful to work with people I respect for their integrity.

53. I am grateful to work with people I admire for their achievements.
54. I use my talents to teach and help others to find success.
55. I follow bliss, not money.
56. I take pride in preparing and educating myself thoroughly so I can do my best.
57. I take advantage of opportunities for professional development without hesitation as they arise.
58. I constantly seek opportunities to further my education and knowledge in my career.
59. I love to get out of my own comfort zone because I know that is where growth happens.
60. I dream big and act fast.
61. My positive habit of regular physical activity has a positive impact on my work.
62. I have the ability to become the

top, most successful person in my field.

63. My positive attitude allows me to get more work done — faster, better, and more efficiently.

64. My enthusiastic attitude drives my success in work and boosts my motivation.

65. I effortlessly remain focused and stay on task in my work.

66. I am proud of how far I have come in my professional journey, and I look forward to going even further.

67. My motivation to do my very best at work is contagious to others that I work with.

68. I approach each day with purpose and passion.

69. I take charge of my life, and I take responsibility for its outcome.

70. I have the energy to work

tirelessly to accomplish the goals that I set for myself.

71. I set a positive example for others through my strong work ethic.

72. I have a clear vision of my own personal version of success.

73. I consistently take the necessary steps for me to reach my goals.

74. My strong and effective communication skills contribute to my career success.

75. I embrace challenges fearlessly and never back down from them.

76. I am constantly checking off goals that I've achieved.

77. My consistent accomplishments make me feel happy, proud, and fulfilled.

78. I think ahead and plan wisely for long-term success in addition to short-term.

79. I put my full effort and energy into everything I do.

80. I keep up with innovation in my field so I can remain ahead of the curve.

81. I always master new technologies in my field so I can remain competitive.

82. I create a positive environment for those I work with.

83. My energy motivates people to work harder, which contributes to our collective success.

84. I surround myself with things that motivate me and keep me inspired.

85. My positivity boosts my energy levels and aids me in being more productive.

86. I am proud to have built a meaningful career that helps contribute to the happiness of others.

87. I am willing to do whatever it takes to pursue and excel in my dream career.

88. I am constantly reaping the benefits of my positive outlook in unexpected ways.
89. I devote my time to complete projects that I start, and my efforts are paying off.
90. I have a can-do attitude, which makes me more productive and efficient with my work.
91. I look forward to working and enjoy what I do.
92. I take advantage of my personal strengths to help me make progress every day.
93. I am unafraid to push myself and I respond well to professional challenges.
94. No matter what, I remain disciplined and keep my eyes on the prize.
95. I am capable of succeeding beyond my wildest imagination in any career path.

96. My hopeful and optimistic outlook makes it easy for opportunities to find me.
97. I am fueled by a sense of purpose, which ensures my success in my endeavors.
98. I feel like a success because I love every part of my life.
99. I commit myself fully to my projects until they are completed with excellence.
100. I am a go-getter, and I take action and go after the things I want in my life.
101. Whatever I see in my mind or visualize in my life, I can attract and attain.
102. I am constantly getting better every day because of my commitment to constant improvement.
103. I go for what I want and expect

the best, regardless of the potential outcomes.

104. The success of others inspires and motivates me.

105. I have incredible self-discipline that causes success in every area of my life.

106. My good attitude and ambition move me closer to prosperity every day.

107. I happily put in time on a consistent basis to realize my goals.

108. My efforts are worth it, and I am constantly rewarded for my persistence.

109. I attain better results in my work by staying motivated.

110. I am surrounded by positive, encouraging people who want success as much as I do.

111. I have the ability to make wise

decisions quickly and follow
through with them quickly.

112. I stay on top of my work and start
and finish things earlier than
planned.

113. I have full faith and unshakeable
confidence that I am able to
achieve my goals.

114. I have wonderful friends, family,
and relationships, which is its own
success.

115. I trust my intuition and follow my
gut instincts because they are
always right.

116. I only see success in my future,
and success is my only option.

117. My past achievements motivate
me to keep pushing forward to
achieve even greater things.

118. I keep my work space clear, which
keeps my mental space clear for
maximum productivity.

119. I make terrific first impressions on

everyone I encounter because of my positive attitude.

120. I possess the necessary traits needed for upward mobility in society and life.

121. I am conscious of the way I mentally and emotionally approach every goal.

122. I know that my attitude has a direct correlation to my performance and outcome.

123. My positive attitude allows me to excel in endeavors both inside and outside of work.

124. I concentrate on big picture thinking and don't get held down by small details.

125. I always go above and beyond the call of duty, for which my efforts are always rewarded.

126. I lead by example and cultivate a positive culture in my workplace.

Accentuating the Positive

1. I am surrounded with positive people.
2. I have a support network of people just as optimistic as I am.
3. I celebrate the little things that make me happy each day and do not dwell on the negative.
4. I have the power to change my mindset and think more positive thoughts.
5. My consistent happiness allows me to improve my creativity and problem-solving skills.

6. I maintain focus on my work and accomplish my goals efficiently because of my positive attitude.

7. I do good things for others, which helps me to be more positive about myself.

8. I focus a little each day on the people, places, and activities that bring me joy.

9. I have control over my own thoughts, and I choose to think positive.

10. I perceive challenges as obstacles to be overcome rather than stumbling blocks to stop me.

11. I spend time every day, examining the positives in my life that bring me joy and gratitude.

12. I think more positively, which causes me to act more positively in my daily interactions.

13. My positive outlook empowers me

to cope well with life changes both big and small.

14. I only consume media with positive messages that empower me and make me feel good.

15. I take pride in taking good care of myself.

16. I enjoy my own company and other people enjoy my company because of my great energy.

17. I take advantage of all the opportunities around me to broaden my cultural horizons.

18. My inexplicable positive energy makes people feel good and gravitate towards me.

19. I stay positive, which allows me to always follow through on my goals.

20. The health of my body is positively affected by the health of my mind.

21. My body stays in great condition

because I keep my mind in great
condition.

22. I am in control of my own destiny
    and I can make any dream of mine
    come true.

23. I choose to possess positive
    emotions and thoughts no matter
    what.

24. I have the power to resolve any
    problem or situation.

25. I can use any obstacle to become a
    better, stronger person.

26. I find the humor in everyday
    situations, which reduces any
    anxiety.

27. I practice positive thinking and
    self-encouragement in small ways
    every day.

28. My positivity makes both my work
    life and my social life more
    enjoyable.

29. I remind myself each day to take
    pride in what I have already done.

30. I always celebrate and give myself credit for my successes.

31. My positive mind frame provides me with energy to exercise at peak physical levels.

32. I have total control over the effort I put into all my endeavors.

33. I have high self-esteem and high self-confidence because of my positive attitude.

34. I take at least one step forward every day to improve my health and well-being.

35. My positivity allows me to handle any situation that comes my way with grace and calmness.

36. My joy for life is magnetic and contagious to those around me.

37. I always live in the moment and enjoy the now.

38. I look at the world in a positive way, which makes people want to be around me.

39. I am at my most beautiful inside and out, when I am happy, positive, and optimistic.
40. I am overwhelmed with the amount of moments in my everyday life that bring me joy.
41. I get better and better each day at coping with life's daily challenges.
42. I always find a way to make someone's day with a kind act or gesture.
43. I am the architect of my own life and the source of my own happiness.
44. I take full responsibility over committing myself to a life of positivity.
45. I fill my life with things that bring me joy.
46. I am surrounded by things that trigger my happiness.
47. Thinking positively builds up my confidence in myself and others.

48. I start each morning positively and remind myself that today will be a good day.
49. I have control over how I experience the present moment, and I choose to be happy now.
50. I constantly remind myself that I am wonderful, capable, and on the right path.
51. I take great care of myself, which further contributes to my overall happiness.
52. I take great care of my possessions, which further contributes to my overall happiness.
53. I take great care of my environment, which further contributes to my overall happiness.
54. I take great care of my relationships, which further

contributes to my overall happiness.

55. When I see others in distress, even if they are a stranger, I make an effort to help uplift them.

56. I take joy in the opportunity to openly praise others for their achievements.

57. I choose to find joy in everything that I do.

58. Happiness and light are a part of who I am and I radiate positivity effortlessly.

59. I take advantage of any opportunity to make someone's day, no matter how small it may seem.

60. I stay focused on the things that I have rather than the things that I do not.

61. I am able to find the positive in any situation.

62. I have control over negative

thoughts and the ability to turn negative thoughts into positive thoughts.

63. I am conditioned to have a habit of reacting positively in any situation.

64. I am mindful of my present thoughts, and able to steer them in a positive direction.

65. I consistently get proper sleep, which helps me feel happier and more refreshed each day.

66. I start off every day with a positive thought so that I begin on the right foot.

67. I forgive others and release grudges to prioritize my personal peace and happiness.

68. I only focus on things I can change instead of obsessing over things I cannot change.

69. I choose to focus on things I can control instead of obsessing over things I cannot control.

70. I make the most of every minute that I have while I am alive.
71. I do what makes me happy and eliminate things that don't make me happy.
72. I always find a way to turn frustrating moments around into positive moments.
73. I grow more and better as a person each and every day.
74. I am an expert at tuning my mindset to the frequency of happiness and positivity.
75. I have successfully retrained my brain to make positive thinking a habit of mine.
76. I have the power to motivate myself to work hard.
77. I have the power to change the way I experience the world by changing the way I perceive it.
78. I listen to my inner voice that

always guides me in the direction of peace.

79. I employ whatever techniques I need to, to free up my mind and concentrate on positive emotions.

80. I am filled with hope and relentless optimism that things will always work out for the best.

81. I focus on the good things in every situation.

82. It brings me joy and happiness to see other people's lives going well for them.

83. With my attitude, I have the power to influence things that happen around me and to me.

84. I always choose the path of positivity.

85. I use my life experiences to help myself and others grow.

86. I give purpose and meaning to my life by pursuing dreams I am passionate about.

87. I speak only words of love and light.
88. I have an unconscious habit of thinking only uplifting thoughts.
89. I measure my own happiness only by my own standards, not other people's standards.
90. I find meaning and growth in any challenging experience that I may face.
91. My positive attitude has a positive impact on every area of my life.
92. Being more positive makes me more attentive and sensitive to the needs of others.
93. I am aware that I am better off than many people in this world, and I can use my position to help others.
94. While I expect the best possible outcomes, I can also handle whatever comes my way.
95. I expect good things to happen to

me on a regular basis, not just by the occasional fluke or stroke of luck.

96. I do my part to contribute to positive outcomes by maintaining a positive attitude.

97. I always think about and discover ways that I can improve a situation.

98. My body and immune system are strong and quick to recover because of my positivity.

99. Things are always looking up and improving for me.

100. I only include myself in conversation that is uplifting, positive, and constructive.

101. I fully appreciate every little thing in my life.

102. I am grateful for the lessons that life is constantly teaching me.

103. I attract positive thoughts and repel negative thoughts.

104. I attract positive emotions and repel negative emotions.

105. I attract positive people and repel negative people.

106. I attract positive experiences and repel negative experiences.

107. I view life as a fun adventure.

108. I always await what's next with excitement and eagerness.

109. My positive attitude is the catalyst that triggers a chain reaction of future successes.

110. I focus on what can be done from this point forward, not on what has already happened.

111. I live in the present and anticipate the future, instead of lamenting over the past.

112. I seek opportunities to acknowledge and appreciate others for their positive outlook.

113. I make a conscious effort to

replace negative thoughts and emotions with positive ones.

114. My positive outlook is bringing more harmony and balance into my life.

115. I go out of my way to make people feel loved and appreciated.

116. My life is looking more promising each and every day.

117. I expect positive outcomes out of my daily interactions.

118. I am convinced that each new day will be greater than the previous one.

119. I seek out opportunities to add more value to my life.

120. I have the capacity to do any seemingly difficult task if I put forth the effort.

121. My positive vibes have a ripple effect that radiate into the world and make it a better place.

122. I think positively, which causes

positive events to take place in my life.

123. I take advantage of the ability I have to make someone's day just by smiling.

124. My positive thinking has opened up a world of new possibilities for me.

125. I constantly smile and laugh, which makes me feel good, and contributes to my good health.

126. I only seek out and attract people who share the same uplifting mindset that I do.

127. I have purpose in my life, which gives each new day meaning and significance.

128. I follow the path that makes me the most happy, not the most money.

129. While I chase happiness instead of money, I know that it is possible to have both.

130. The songs I choose to listen to are upbeat and uplifting.

131. The content I choose to watch boosts my mood and calms my mind.

132. I prioritize spending time in nature because it brings me serenity and peace, making optimism effortless.

133. My positivity allows me to experience continual growth in my work and personal life.

134. I find happiness and comfort in supporting and loving others.

135. I find happiness and comfort in being supported and loved.

136. I have a clear vision of my happiest self and I take strides daily to make that vision a reality.

137. No matter what I want, I know I can find a way to get it.

Relationships & Supporting Others

1. I foster supportive, loving relationships which increase my long-term happiness.
2. I love myself for who I am, and I accept others for who they are.
3. My optimistic attitude allows me to build good relationships and strong friendships.
4. I treat myself and others with compassion and kindness.
5. I treat my family and friends with love that uplifts and encourages them.

6. I attract healthy and happy personal relationships by projecting a positive attitude.
7. I surround myself with positive people and have an optimistic and reliable network of support.
8. I make others around me happier through my positive attitude.
9. I use empathy and sympathy to support others in their times of need.
10. My positive outlook contributes to my success in my relationships and my overall life.
11. I have an infectious laugh and smile that improves the moods of people around me.
12. I possess willpower and self-control, which positively benefits my romantic and social relationships.
13. I surprise strangers and the people

in my life with random acts of kindness to brighten their day.

14. I encourage my family and friends to do well because I want to see them at their best.

15. I am respectful of viewpoints and opinions that are different from my own.

16. My agreeable and happy disposition strengthen my connections with others.

17. I grow more and more empathetic every day.

18. My positive outlook attracts positive friends, which contributes to further happiness.

19. I am fortunate to have close personal and professional relationships that make me happy.

20. I openly share my thoughts and feelings with my loved ones.

21. My openness with my feelings

relieves stress and makes me feel stronger emotionally.

22. I am able to remain positive and optimistic no matter who I am around.
23. I am encouraging to others when they are in need of a mood boost.
24. I am easily able to be patient with my friends, family, and partner.
25. The patience I possess strengthens the emotional bonds in my relationships.
26. My positive attitude is contagious to all who come in contact with me.
27. I support my significant other, friends and family whenever I can because it makes them happy to know I care.
28. I treat others the way I want to be treated myself.
29. I am happier when I have stronger

social connections and familial bonds.

30. My positive relationships with friends and family positively contribute to my self-confidence.

31. I value the quality of my relationships with my partner, friends, and family.

32. I provide support and unconditional love to myself and to those around me.

33. All of my relationships with friends, family, and loved ones are built on trust, honesty, and loyalty.

34. I make an effort to create and nourish positive relationships and get to know people better.

35. My close relationships contribute to increased happiness for both me and the other people involved.

36. I radiate and project positive energy, which attracts high quality people and relationships to me.

37. I relish the moments that I spend with my partner, friends, and family.
38. I put effort into creating opportunities to strengthen the bonds between me and the people I love.
39. I love laughing with my loved ones because it is good for my mental and physical health.
40. I am there for my social and personal connections when they need me.
41. I make an effort to do things for my partner, friends, and family that make them happy.
42. My passion and positivity inspire others around me to feel joy and happiness.
43. I happily celebrate and recognize the successes of my peers.
44. I make myself available to talk to

Think Happy Thoughts Affirmations and Meditation for...

and emotionally support my loved ones whenever they need me.

45. I build trust in my personal and work relationships by delivering on my promises.

46. I freely give compliments to others to improve their happiness, outlook and self-esteem.

47. I form and nurture relationships by creating and participating in social events regularly.

48. I interact more with people who matter most in my life, than I do with screens and electronic devices.

49. I voluntarily reach out to others and offer help even if they have not asked me for it.

50. I make an effort to be considerate of the happiness of others.

51. I expand other people's networks by bringing people together.

52. I create opportunities for me and

59

my loved ones to enjoy doing
things together that we love.

53. I work well with others in
professional environments.

54. I have strong connections with the
people I work with.

55. I make an effort to regularly call
the people I love and remind them
that I care.

56. I always find thoughtful ways to
show my significant other that I
care.

57. I share things that make me happy
with other people so it can also
make them happy and brighten
their day.

58. I make an effort to meet new
people with shared interests.

59. My time is my most valuable asset,
and I show others I love them
when I choose to spend it with
them.

60. I use my talents and ideas to help others.

61. I strengthen my relationships when I share my gifts with others, rather than keep them to myself.

62. I sometimes make healthy sacrifices for the people close to me in order to make them happy.

63. I make an effort to dedicate time to talking and listening to my partner, friends, and family.

64. I make myself emotionally available to my loved ones.

65. I openly express gratitude to my loved ones to thank them for all they've done for me.

66. Whenever I am with a loved one, I am fully physically, mentally, and emotionally present.

67. I constantly look for and discover ways to connect with people over similar interests.

68. I look for ways to help others to

decrease their stress and lessen their burdens.

69. I look for ways to help make other people happier.
70. I acknowledge the importance of communication in any successful relationship.
71. I am constantly working on improving my communication skills.
72. I spontaneously plan fun, shared experiences with my loved ones to bring us closer.
73. I am there for my loved ones in times of sickness and in health.
74. I am a reliable source of positive energy to others in their darkest times of need.
75. I let my loved ones know I care through my actions as well as my words.
76. I take joy in creating opportunities to bring others joy.

77. No matter how busy I get, I always set aside time for the people I love.
78. I make an effort to be sensitive to the needs of my partner, friends, and family.
79. My life is more fulfilling because of my wonderful relationships.
80. I am positive and encouraging to everyone, which makes people love being around me.
81. I offer positive and constructive feedback to people without being negative or overly critical.
82. I amplify my enjoyment of the things I love by sharing them with the people I love.
83. I do good things for others without being asked.
84. I am a strong, positive influence on others, and I help people cultivate a positive mindset.
85. My relationships are more

important to me than material
possessions.

86. I make an effort to provide
emotional support for others when
they are not at their best.
87. I am fun to be around because I
am happy.
88. I make an effort not to isolate
myself because being around
others brings me joy.
89. I am a ray of sunshine, who
brightens other's people's days
when they are feeling down.
90. I find that I am happier in my
romantic relationships because of
my optimism.
91. I am able to provide emotional
support for other people and still
maintain my positivity and
optimism at the same time.
92. I find and share positive solutions
to other people's problems with
ease.

93. My high emotional intelligence allows me to better understand the needs of others.

94. It is easy for me to constantly meet new people and cultivate new friendships.

95. I enjoy meeting people from different backgrounds because it makes me more empathetic and open minded.

96. I believe in my partner, friends, and family and I motivate them to do and achieve their best.

97. My effortlessly social nature and positive attitude make it easy for me to meet people for romantic relationships.

98. My effortlessly social nature and positive attitude make it easy for me to meet people for platonic relationships.

99. I recognize that everyone is entitled to their own opinion.

100. I accept people who think and believe differently than I do.
101. I respect the privacy and personal time for both me and the people I am in relationships with.
102. I keep an open mind and avoid being judgmental of others.
103. I know that good relationships take work and I am willing and able to happily put the work in.
104. My positive attitude provides strength and longevity for my relationships.
105. I take good care of myself, which helps me more easily attract good romantic and platonic relationships.
106. I always find time and ways to send positive messages to the people I love and care about.
107. I accept my loved ones for who they are and respect their opinions that differ from my own.

108. I accept my loved ones for who they are and respect their choices that differ from my own.

109. I am able to communicate my feelings in positive and constructive ways.

110. I choose to only spend time in my life with supportive, positive, and uplifting people.

111. I make an effort to fully show up in my life and relationships.

112. I accept myself, which allows me to accept others.

113. I have a strong professional network that supports and contributes to my career success.

114. I make an effort to make gestures, big and small, to show love for my loved ones.

115. I have a romantic partner who fully supports and loves me, and I do the same for them.

116. I sometimes put my own desires

aside and do things I don't want to do because I know it is important to a person I love.

117. I am always honest because trust is the foundation of my personal relationships.

Gratitude

1. I keep an inventory of things I am grateful for every single day.
2. My happiness and mental state are improved because I express gratitude regularly.
3. I am grateful to have family and friends in my life who love and support me.
4. I am thankful that expressing gratitude allows me to tap into a well of positive emotions.
5. I appreciate that gratitude and

love can boost my self-worth and self-confidence.

6. I am grateful for the level of education and wisdom that I have attained thus far.

7. I appreciate the ability gratitude has to strengthen my personal relationships.

8. I am fortunate to have gratitude, because it gives me a brighter, more optimistic outlook.

9. I am grateful for the chance to make a positive difference in the lives of others in both big and small ways.

10. I appreciate that I have the opportunity to work hard and improve the lives of others.

11. I am grateful for my health and a sound mind.

12. I am fortunate to have family and friends who are there for me when I need help and support.

13. I am grateful for each day that I have in this world.

14. I appreciate my insatiable curiosity and childlike wonder for life.

15. I am grateful to see life in a way that is always interesting and enjoyable.

16. I enjoy every bit of my life's journey, and appreciate even the small moments of joy it brings.

17. I am grateful to have empathy and compassion for the predicaments of others.

18. I am grateful to be able to relate to the feelings of others, as it makes my human connections stronger.

19. I am grateful that no matter how much or how little I have, I always have something to give or help others with.

20. I am grateful for the opportunity to spend time with people who make me feel happy.

21. I appreciate the generosity of my family, friends, and partner that enhance my life.
22. My immense gratitude that I feel makes me humble, and makes me appreciate everything I have.
23. I am fortunate to have a good sense of humor that helps brighten my days.
24. I am fortunate to have a happy disposition that helps brighten the lives of those around me.
25. I am grateful for the connectedness of the world and the opportunity to travel to enjoy different cultures and experiences.
26. I am grateful for the internet and the endless, convenient source of knowledge that it provides.
27. I am grateful to live in a time where information is freely available at the click of a button.
28. I am grateful to have personal

freedom to express myself the way
I want.

29. I am grateful to live in a free
society where I can conduct my
life the way I want.

30. I am grateful expressing my
gratitude improves my health and
emotional well-being.

31. I am thankful for all my personal
teachers who have shown up along
the way and made a positive
difference in my life.

32. I appreciate that feeling gratitude
reduces stress and anxiety.

33. I am grateful for the opportunity
to nurture my existing
relationships.

34. I am thankful for the diversity and
beauty in nature.

35. I am fortunate to have experienced
the kindness of others.

36. I am grateful that you don't need a
lot of money to be happy.

37. I am thankful that the best things in life are free.
38. Feelings of gratitude create feelings of happiness, and happiness leads to success.
39. I am grateful that this world is filled with beauty that costs me nothing to experience and enjoy.
40. I am grateful that sunshine always follows every storm.
41. I appreciate the opportunity to experience things I already love, and also discover new things.
42. I am thankful for the simple moments I can share with the special people in my life.
43. I am grateful for the time I have to spend with the loved ones who matter most.
44. I am fortunate to have honest and loyal, close friends and family.
45. I feel grateful for all the

experiences that bring me lasting moments of joy.

46. I appreciate the selflessness of people who work in service jobs that enhance my quality of life.

47. I appreciate the people who don't even know me who work every day to keep me safe.

48. I appreciate the selflessness of everyday heroes who sacrifice their own personal freedom in order to protect mine.

49. I am thankful for all the positive memories I have accumulated over my lifetime of experiences.

50. I am grateful for positive memories that help me vividly and joyously remember loved ones even after they are gone.

51. I am grateful that there is always something amazing to look forward to in my life.

52. I feel grateful for my strength and ability to overcome adversity.
53. I am grateful for the power to forgive and for the forgiveness of others.
54. I appreciate the parents, guardians, and mentors that have instilled positive values in me.
55. I am grateful for the parental figures in my life who have looked out for my best interest and ensured that I was on the right path.
56. I am thankful for the free opportunity every day to experience beautiful sunrises and sunsets.
57. I am grateful that even if I do not have a lot of money that I can always give of my time to make someone else's life better.
58. I appreciate the guidance and

wisdom dispensed to me by my
family and my mentors.

59. I am fortunate to have people in
    my life to lend me a helping hand.
60. I am grateful to be surrounded by
    ambitious and talented people who
    inspire and motivate me.
61. I feel grateful for the feelings of
    benevolence that motivate me to
    do good things for others.
62. I appreciate artists who dedicate
    their lives to sharing their talents
    by creating images, music, and
    media that I can enjoy.
63. I am thankful for the relaxing
    sounds of nature that I can
    experience any time for free just
    by going outside.
64. I appreciate the healing power of
    music and how easily accessible
    it is.
65. I am grateful to have easy access

to information and documentaries
that open my mind.

66. I am grateful for being surrounded
by new ways of looking at things.
67. I am fortunate to have the ability
to communicate my feelings and
concerns with others.
68. I am grateful for the ability to
spend quality time with the people
I love.
69. I am thankful to be able to support
my health with both modern and
natural medicine.
70. I appreciate all weather because I
know that all seasons serve a
purpose.
71. I am grateful for pets and animals,
and their ability to instantly
cultivate feelings of joy and love.
72. I am fortunate to feel hopeful for a
brighter future.
73. I am thankful for the holidays that

bring my family and friends together.

74. I appreciate all the gifts I have received throughout the years from thoughtful people.

75. I appreciate the sensation of a warm shower on a cold morning.

76. I am grateful for a warm jacket on a winter night.

77. I am grateful for a warm cup of tea on a cold evening.

78. I am grateful for a cool shower on a hot day.

79. I am grateful to have power and control over my mind.

80. I am thankful to have my mental health and emotional well-being.

81. I am grateful for the power and ability I have to set goals and achieve them.

82. I am thankful for the strength and resilience to carry on after temporary setbacks.

83. I am fortunate to have shelter and to have a roof over my head.

84. I am grateful to have access to transportation and the ability to get around to where I need to go.

85. I appreciate the true heroes out there who put their lives at risk to save others.

86. I feel grateful for the simple pleasures in life like fresh new flowers blooming in spring.

87. I appreciate the changing of the seasons and the burst of vivid color in the fall.

88. I am fortunate to be alive, and I make the most of every single day I am given.

89. I appreciate moments of solitude that bring me inner peace.

90. I appreciate moments of communion with others who bring me happiness.

91. I am grateful for the opportunity to learn from my experiences.

92. I am thankful for those who use their beautiful words to inspire me and others.

93. I am grateful for the endless career possibilities that I have.

94. I am grateful to have the ability to turn my life around in any moment that I choose to.

95. I am grateful to be able to make my life into anything that I want it to be.

96. I feel fortunate to have loved ones who know just what to say or do to cheer me up.

97. I appreciate that there are people who care enough to ask me how I am doing.

98. I am grateful for all the hobbies and interests that I am passionate about.

99. I am thankful for all of the

successes I have had so far in my life.

100. I feel fortunate for all the happy moments I have to cherish.

101. I feel grateful that positive thinking is always a choice available to me.

102. I am thankful for the days when I can unplug and unwind.

103. I am grateful that after the winter, spring always returns, bringing forth new life and beauty.

104. I feel fortunate to live a life filled with meaning and purpose.

105. I am thankful for the chance to become part of something bigger than myself.

106. I appreciate finding pleasant moments when they are least expected.

107. I am already grateful for the amazing moments that are coming in my future.

108. I am thankful to be able to use every experience in my life to make me a better person.

109. I am thankful to be able to use every experience in my life to teach others to be better people.

110. I am grateful for the nutrition and deliciousness that food provides to make me look and feel good.

111. I appreciate the freedom I have to choose my own path in life.

112. I appreciate every compliment I receive from others to brighten my day.

113. I am thankful for the ability to envision success and the conviction to follow through and make it happen.

114. I feel grateful that there are always opportunities available to me to better myself.

115. I appreciate having access to conveniences I often take for

granted like clean drinking water, indoor plumbing, and electricity.

116. I am grateful to have enough food to maintain the health and nourishment of my body.

117. I make an effort to thank every single person who has made a positive impact on my life.

118. I am thankful for all the adventures I have embarked upon.

119. I feel grateful for kind gestures from the random strangers that I meet.

120. I feel fortunate for the overflowing happiness that I have to offer others.

121. I am grateful for every day I wake up to greet the sunrise.

122. I appreciate the satisfied feeling that comes with an honest day's hard work.

123. I am thankful for all the special

things, big and small, that make
life worth living.

124. I am grateful that something as
simple as saying "thank you" can
lead to happiness.

125. I feel grateful to live in a time
where I can instantly and easily
communicate with my friends,
family, and loved ones.

126. I appreciate my daily routines that
start and end my days off right.

127. I am grateful for the quality
content that other people have
shared on the internet that opens
my mind to new things.

128. I am grateful for a time of rest
after a time of work.

129. I am thankful to have people in my
life who love me unconditionally.

130. I appreciate my freedom to be
myself and express my
individuality.

131. I am grateful for the technological

innovations that make my life more convenient.

132. I am grateful for my ability to laugh and quickly move forward from a bad situation.

133. I feel fortunate for all the role models who have served as a positive influence in my life.

134. I am thankful for the wisdom I gain from others who have already experienced what I am going through.

135. I am grateful for my ability to find the silver lining in everything.

136. I am thankful for life's teachable moments that provide me with valuable lessons.

137. I appreciate overcast days because they make me even more grateful for sunny weather.

Optimism

1. I live by the idea that optimism is contagious and I am always spreading it wherever I go.
2. I harness the power of my optimism to achieve the goals that I set for myself.
3. I am confident that I can overcome adversity and any obstacles that try to get in the way of me accomplishing my goals.
4. I make others happy and more productive by projecting my own optimism.

5. My relentless optimism increases my levels of happiness and improves my chances of success.
6. I practice random acts of kindness that benefit my own well-being and that of others.
7. I am optimistic that things are always going to work out for the best for me.
8. My hard work and persistence pay off and will continue to pay off.
9. I do what I love and bring passion to every moment of my life, and my enthusiasm inspires others.
10. If I do not get something that I want, I know it is because there is something even better out there for me.
11. I grow more and more optimistic every day.
12. Every day, I get closer and closer to becoming the best version of myself.

13. I follow my dreams with the conviction that everything is going to work out for me.

14. I smile constantly, and it makes myself and people around me feel good.

15. I manage stress with ease because I possess an optimistic attitude.

16. I am confident that tomorrow will be even better than today.

17. My good health can be greatly attributed to my unfailing optimism.

18. My persistence and dedication guarantee my wealth and prosperity.

19. I take calculated risks fearlessly because I know the eventual rewards for my efforts far outweigh any apparent risks.

20. I am constantly moving forward and excelling in my career and personal development.

21. My optimistic outlook on life improves my social and romantic relationships.
22. I always find a way to perceive events and outcomes in a positive light.
23. My optimism gives me peace in the life decisions that I make, no matter how big or small.
24. I teach and show others how to think and react positively in all situations.
25. My optimistic attitude allows me to be more productive in my work.
26. Things are going great in my life and they will only continue to get even better.
27. My optimistic attitude allows me to better support and encourage my loved ones.
28. I am able to find humor in all situations, no matter how bad they may seem.

29. I possess the strength of character
to choose a more productive path
for myself.

30. I achieve greater positive results in
my daily life just by maintaining a
positive attitude.

31. I always have the power to choose
my response in every situation,
and I always choose to react
positively.

32. I have the mental fortitude to stay
on top of any situation without
overwhelm.

33. I push self-doubt aside, and do not
allow it to get between me and my
dreams.

34. I constantly look forward when
chasing my goals and do not dwell
on past mistakes.

35. My effortlessly positive demeanor
helps shape my identity as an
optimistic person.

36. I always surround myself with

optimistic people and we feed off of each other's optimism.

37. I approach each new day with a positive mindset.

38. By doing favors for others, I encourage those around me to "pay it forward," sparking a chain of positivity.

39. I share my knowledge with people who can benefit from my guidance and expertise.

40. I always give words of encouragement and support to my family, peers, and co-workers.

41. I study and mimic optimistic people and how they respond to conflict and crisis.

42. While I possess strong self-discipline, I sometimes change up my routines to do something different and maintain excitement in my life.

43. I am resilient in the face of any

struggles that may arise on the road to pursuing my dreams.

44. I am passionate about my career.

45. I am constantly making professional strides forward towards greater fulfilment and prosperity.

46. I am constantly rewiring my brain for positivity and optimism.

47. I possess the calmness and the poise to handle high pressure situations well.

48. I am excited about attaining my own personal version of success.

49. I am confident that I can achieve anything with hard work and grit.

50. I take action to make changes in my life and don't wait for someone else to change it for me.

51. I believe in my vision for myself, and I stay committed to following through no matter what.

52. I am surrounded with confident

and competent people who help
reinforce my positive can-do
attitude.

53. I put my focus on planning for a
brighter future, which allows me
to move on from the past.

54. I have control over my attitude
and outlook, and they, in turn,
influence my actions.

55. I expend the necessary effort to
maintain an optimistic viewpoint
because I know the positive
outcomes are worth it.

56. My constant mental fixation on
success will become a self-fulfilling
prophecy.

57. I have the ability to improvise and
think of good solutions quickly, on
my feet.

58. I feel secure knowing that
contentment and joy are always
available to me, and all I have to
do is continue to seek them out.

59. I always see the positive in the world where others see the negative.
60. By possessing and exhibiting an optimistic worldview, I serve as a role model to others.
61. I compliment others more than I complain about them.
62. Living with joy is a conscious choice that I always make.
63. I always choose to see the best in other people.
64. My life is exciting and consistently presenting me with opportunities of which I will take advantage.
65. I laugh loud and often.
66. I make an effort to find solutions, not blame.
67. I know I will do great at anything I do because I prepare well for every task in front of me.
68. My positive and optimistic outlook

contributes to greater health and longer life.

69. People love to be around me and have relationships with me because I am optimistic.

70. I keep my attention on what goes right, and not what goes wrong.

71. My optimistic outlook helps me to see the abundant possibilities available to me.

72. I continue pressing forward no matter what because persistence pays off and effort is rewarded.

73. I concentrate on the reasons why I *can* accomplish something.

74. I am doing well, my life is great, and I continue improving myself in some way every day.

75. I have tremendous satisfaction in my career and I thoroughly enjoy what I do.

76. I strive to be a positive example

and a source of inspiration for others.

77. I perceive challenges as perfect opportunities for personal development.

78. If one door closes, another even better door of opportunity will open for me.

79. I proactively make positive changes in my life and do not sit around waiting for good things to happen.

80. I take advantage of the wonderful opportunities that come my way.

81. I choose to perceive the good as a permanent fixture and the bad as a temporary inconvenience.

82. I enjoy the present more because I am optimistic.

83. I know that I have an amazing future ahead of me.

84. I feel immense satisfaction with my life.

85. I am hopeful and faithful that things are getting better all the time.
86. I only allow people around me who are cheerful, bright, and happy.
87. No matter what another person's response is, I am in control of my own.
88. I do not allow other people's reactions to events to dictate my own reactions.
89. My positive attitude allows me to make an impact on the world around me.
90. I expect good things to happen to me, through me, and for me.
91. I anticipate happiness and success for myself, which allows me to easily overcome any obstacles that may arise.
92. My optimism gives me the energy and motivation to solve problems.

93. I choose to focus my mind and thoughts on what I want to happen.

94. I am constantly planting the seeds of a positive lifestyle, therefore, I will harvest the rewards.

95. No matter what the situation, there is always something I can do to change it.

96. I choose to leave negative thinking behind and instead blaze a happiness trail.

97. My genuine smile has a ripple effect that spreads joy out into the world.

98. I approach problems with a solution oriented mindset.

99. I am the captain of my thought ship, and I only steer myself toward positive seas.

100. I am humble and grateful, which attracts even more things for me to be grateful for.

101. I offer solutions instead of complaints.
102. I know that there is a solution to every perceived problem.
103. I feel empowered by my ability to control my own optimism and happiness levels.
104. I choose to live only with people who are positive and happy, and our positivity influences one another.
105. I have a relaxed and loving atmosphere in my home, which fills me and everyone who enters it with happiness.
106. It is always worth the effort to train my mind to be more optimistic.
107. I always maintain sight of my desired outcomes for my career and personal life.
108. I am mindful of which of my

thoughts are helpful and which
need to be discarded.

109. I believe that with optimism,
anything is possible.

Healthy Happy Habits, Healthy Happy Life

1. I always look at every situation from a positive point of view.
2. I acknowledge and embrace my emotions in a healthy way.
3. My optimism and positivity lead me to an improved state of well-being.
4. I have a sound body and sound mind because I take care of myself by eating well and exercising.
5. I have a reputation for always looking on the bright side of things.

6. I have a zest for life and an appreciation for all things big and small.
7. My body is a temple, and I treat it with respect.
8. I set and achieve exercise goals for myself regularly.
9. I am getting physically stronger with each passing day.
10. I incorporate productive and helpful physical and mental activities into my daily life.
11. I do things every day to help me relax, reduce stress, and stay healthy.
12. I always overcome any doubts that may cross my mind and focus instead on the possibilities.
13. I listen to my body and stay on top of my healthcare needs.
14. I often make an effort to go into nature and enjoy the peace and serenity that it brings.

15. Every day, I rewire my brain a little bit more for positive thoughts.
16. I have responsible spending habits.
17. I use my money for things that contribute to better health and a sound mind.
18. I make progress each day to replace unhealthy habits with healthy alternatives.
19. I regularly support others in need by giving my time and money to worthy causes.
20. I always see tasks that I start to completion.
21. I always lighten a heavy mood with humor and optimism.
22. I stick to the decisions I make to change and benefit my health, which include both exercise and diet.
23. I practice self-discipline, self-

control, and moderation with my consumption of things.

24. I do what's best for the long term outcome, instead of succumbing to instant gratification.

25. I am goal-oriented, but I always make time for a fun activity or adventure every day.

26. I exercise my power to create my own happiness through my thoughts and actions.

27. I do whatever it takes to keep my mind fixed on positivity.

28. I keep my living and working spaces clean and neat because it keeps my mind clear and at peace.

29. Every day, I put good, nutritious foods in my body that have a positive impact on my health and energy.

30. I always find a way to brighten someone else's day in a small way,

even if it is someone I do not yet know.

31. I always put effort into creating opportunities for fun, unique life experiences that will establish happy memories.

32. I always focus on the big picture and don't sweat the small stuff.

33. I always make sure that I get good quality sleep so I can maintain sharp focus and a brighter mood.

34. I exercise physical and mental control over any vices or bad habits.

35. I regularly audit my habits and patterns to determine what unhelpful actions I should eliminate from my behavior.

36. I regularly find ways to incorporate new, good habits in ways that make them stick for the long run.

37. I regularly release and process my

emotions in my own healthy and productive ways so things don't build up.

38. I find healthy ways every day to release endorphins that make me feel happy and exhilarated.

39. I approach lifestyle changes with small, manageable increments so I can handle it more effectively.

40. I take small consistent action towards my goals to increase my chance of success.

41. I always make decisions keeping in mind the best interest of my future self.

42. Every day in every way, I always replace bad with good, and negative with positive.

43. I balance my life with the discipline of routine and the fun of spontaneity.

44. I have an excellent morning routine that makes me more

productive and positive
throughout the entire day.

45. I actively control my days, instead of being reactive to whatever comes up.

46. I keep track of my goals and my progress, which increases my chances of success.

47. I take time every day away from technology, the internet, and social media to clear and calm my mind.

48. I purposefully fill my life with things that make me smile.

49. I only bring things into my space that fill me with joy.

50. I spend more time creating than consuming.

51. I make a habit of following through on the goals I set for myself.

52. I work hard and give 110 percent to everything I do.

53. I always make time to treat myself

and reward myself for my hard
work.

54. I give more compliments than
criticism.

55. I always find ways to invest in
bettering myself and promoting
my self-improvement.

56. I make an effort to regularly
connect with the people I love and
enjoy.

57. I condition myself to think more
positively about the state of the
world and the people in it.

58. I take time every day to increase
my intelligence and make myself
more well-informed.

59. I always find new skills and
hobbies to learn to increase my
confidence and discipline.

60. I have a night routine that allows
me to end the day on the right
foot.

61. I exercise control over the things I

put in my body and the amount of them.

62. I seek out ways to motivate myself and incorporate those tactics into my daily life.

63. I always watch and listen to inspirational and motivational content to boost my mood, faith, and willpower.

64. I always choose happiness.

65. I practice positive self-talk and encourage myself to continue moving forward.

66. I reframe every event if I have to until I see it as positive.

67. I cherish and celebrate life's happy moments as they come along.

68. I always handle my moods and the moods of others well, which helps me grow as a person.

69. I provide mental and emotional support to those in need.

70. I have a habit of excellence.

71. I always put all of my very best into everything I do in every area of my life.
72. I put conscious effort into cultivating positive habits that translate into life successes.
73. I express gratitude daily and appreciate all the things that I have.
74. I have a habit of happiness, which allows me to effortlessly think positively.
75. I stimulate my mind daily with challenges that sharpen and improve my brain function.
76. I tap into my mind's ability to refocus so I can consistently block out the negative.
77. I repeat positive thoughts and actions daily until they become ingrained in me.
78. I find ways to improve challenging situations rather than avoid them.

79. I limit the distractions around me so I can be more productive.
80. I hold myself accountable for reaching the goals I set for myself.
81. I always prepare for tomorrow, today, to maximize my productivity.
82. I take my nutrition and health seriously and always seek and employ ways to improve both.
83. I always find a way for me to relax and unwind each day so that I am better equipped to start the next day fully re-energized.
84. I think outside of the box on how to approach challenges.
85. I remain in control of my mood no matter what other people say or do around me.
86. I think happy thoughts until it becomes second nature.
87. I seek and find ways to discover peace of mind daily.

88. I make sure to remain flexible so that I can continue to grow as a person.
89. I actively seek out opportunities to explore hobbies that interest and excite me.
90. I always choose kind and caring thoughts.
91. I make wise life decisions.
92. I invest the time and energy necessary to become a more positive thinker.
93. I repeat positive statements until they become positive actions.
94. I manage stress and anxiety in healthy and productive ways.
95. I always look for opportunities to give other people things to be grateful for.
96. I maintain healthy sleeping patterns to improve my mental clarity and sharpness.

97. I choose to focus my attention on media that motivates and inspires.

98. I release negativity and forgive others easily to protect my positive, optimistic outlook.

99. I take responsibility for the things that happen to me in my life.

100. I constantly remind myself that I always have a choice.

101. When I want something, I go for it.

102. I live with no excuses and no regrets.

All by Drew McArthur on
Amazon & Audible

Affirmations, Meditation, & Hypnosis For Positivity & A Success Mindset:

*Power Of Thought To Create A Millionaire Mind,
Manifest Wealth, Abundance, Better Relationships, &
Form Positive Habits Now*

**Rewire Your Brain Affirmations, Meditation,
& Hypnosis For Confidence, Motivation, &
Discipline:**

*Increase Focus, Productivity, Willpower, Self Esteem,
& Eliminate Distraction & Procrastination Habits*

**Step-By-Step Motivational Goal Setting
Course For Life Mastery:**

*How To Change Your Brain, Set Your Vision, And
Get Everything You Want To Have Your Best
Year Ever*

Monkey Mind Cure Affirmations, Meditation & Hypnosis:

How to Stop Worrying, Kill Fear, Rewire Your Brain, and Change Your Anxious Thoughts to Start Living a Stress and Anxiety-Free Life

Think Happy Thoughts: Affirmations and Meditation for Positive Thinking, Learned Optimism and a Happy Brain

Unlock the Advantage of the Happiness Habit and Project the Power of Positive Energy

Millionaire Money Mindset: Affirmations, Meditation, & Hypnosis

Using Positive Thinking Psychology to Train Your Mind to Grow Wealth, Think like the New Rich and Take the Secret Fastlane to Success

CPSIA information can be obtained
at www.ICGtesting.com
Printed in the USA
FSHW020902050520
69872FS

9 781650 216881